COLORISM

Essays & Poems

Edited by: Sarah L. Webb
ColorismHealing.org

ISBN-13: 978-1976293276
ISBN-10: 1976293278

Dedication

This book is dedicated to all the girls and boys, women and men, wounded by colorism, who seek a space to give voice to their pain, and to those who search for a space to journey through the healing process with a loving and compassionate community.

Acknowledgments

This book was made possible by all 2017 CHWC contestants, judges Alejandra Torres and Amaris Wilson, Black Women Being fund, Alysia Fields and Toni Point of Statement Goods Design, and a host of other supporters.

TABLE OF CONTENTS

ESSAYS

POEMS

REFLECTION

Fair Weather

Sarah L. Webb

c. 1997

It took a while for me to remember
That rainy, gray morning in September
A girl with skin like the sun
Didn't stop me from having fun
A lot of attention is what she got
Friends try to bring me along
I say I would rather not
Because right here the will is strong
The two of us they try to compare
But I'm used to it, so I don't care
I don't care if her hair is long
With my hair I see nothing wrong
So what if I have darker skin
I'm not deprived of any finesse
And might I say again
It adds to my gracefulness
The guys try to put her in my place
Because they claim she has a prettier face
But I can, without the slightest hint of a try,
See myself as beautiful until I die

Introduction

"unless the question of Colorism—in my definition, prejudicial or preferential treatment of same-race people based solely on their color—is addressed in our communities and definitely in our black 'sisterhoods' we cannot, as a people, progress. For colorism, like colonialism, sexism, and racism, impedes us"
Alice Walker

I wrote the poem "Fair Weather" when I was in middle school approximately twenty years ago. I don't remember ever discussing the subject with others, but I'd felt the dull pressure, the sometimes sharp burn of colorism since before my conscious recollection (according to the story my mother recalls). I've possibly been impacted by colorism in a sequence of atomic waves since my conception (or even prior to that!) from womb into womanhood.

When I decided to launch the first writing contest in 2013, I published this poem on the CH blog, my first time sharing it with a public audience. One reason I host the contest is to give people the kind of platform I would have benefited from. Rather than writing poems and tucking them away in notebooks, never to be seen by anyone, this contest gives people the chance to offer their expressions to a wider world.

What I hope these collections will show is the diversity of ideas and experiences of colorism, as well as the similarities. The contest serves as a prompt to get people really thinking about colorism–what it means, why it exists, how it operates, how it makes them or others feel, how it affects individual lives and entire societies.

The professional, career writer in me could make a thousand revisions and edits to this poem, but I left it as it was originally written, true to who I was at that time. The poem is a peek into what's driven me over the years to eventually dedicate myself to this work of colorism healing.

* * *

Colorism is prejudice based on skin tone and features such as eye color, hair texture, or size and shape of one's nose and lips. People most commonly use the term colorism when describing prejudice among those of the same race, but it also occurs between different races and ethnicities. Alice Walker coined the term colorism in her 1983 book, *In Search of Our Mothers' Gardens*. However, people have written about this global phenomenon for at least a century, using other terms to describe it such as skin-tone bias, pigmentocracy, shadeism, color struck, and the color complex.

Colorism affects the lives of individuals on both personal and societal levels. Research studies and personal testimonies show that colorism is linked to inequalities or lack of visibility and representation in: media, marriage, income and wealth, employment, education, healthcare, and in the criminal justice system. Colorism can also have negative effects on one's psychological wellbeing, contributing to depression and low self-esteem. In each of these areas, people with lighter skin generally fare better than those with darker skin. The collected works in this volume convey the ways colorism ultimately hurts everyone—people of all shades, whole families, communities, and entire societies. At the same time, these essays and poems can serve as a soothing salve to ease emotional injuries and as a cardinal compass that points toward healing.

In July 2013, I created the blog Colorism Healing with the mission to help break the generational cycle of colorism around the world. Within that first year, I noticed several of the blog's visitors were searching for poems about colorism. After scouring the Internet myself, I realized how difficult it was to find poems that directly addressed this topic. As a solution, I launched the Colorism Healing Poetry Contest (CHPC) to generate poems that would be published online for the world to read. In 2017, I opened the contest to include essay submissions as well, and changed the name to the Colorism Healing Writing Contest (CHWC).

Over 800 writers have submitted to the contest since its 2014 launch. The contestants represent diverse ages, regions, ethnicities, languages, styles, and perspectives. Throughout the years, I have had the honor of working with amazing guest judges, including award-winning authors such as Sharon G. Flake and Opal Palmer Adisa, successful artists and writers like Calida Rawles and Amaris Wilson, and talented scholars and advocates like Dr. JeffriAnne Wilder, Alejandra Torres, and Kiara Lee. Contest awards include cash prizes and publication online at ColorismHealing.org and/or in print through books like this one.

The CHWC helps achieve the mission to increase awareness of colorism among all people and to promote personal and communal healing. That healing can happen for the writers as they publicly testify about the truth of their lives, and it can happen for readers as we witness these truths.

"*I have come to believe over and over again that what is most important to me must be spoken, made verbal and shared, even at the risk of having it bruised or misunderstood*"
–Audre Lorde

ESSAYS

Yo Daddy's Side

Ebonie Adams

Growing up in low income housing a.k.a. "The Hood," everyone faced the same struggles. Black people were the majority. It was comfortable, it was Home. It wasn't until I was in middle school, when I left "The Hood," that I realized I was different. And that all black people weren't built the same.

I was the black girl with the "white voice." I never knew what a white voice was or why my skin made it so hard for the two to connect. It was a known fact that I took after my "daddy's side." Meaning that I was dark skinned. I just never thought that taking after "yo daddy's side" would be so difficult.

I remember a girl (who was also black) telling me that I looked like a monkey. At 10 years old, it didn't bother me because I didn't understand the negativity behind the words. I remember going home to tell my mom what happened. But something stopped me. I was staring at her face and was disgusted. Someone I always thought was strong and beautiful was suddenly ugly to me. At that moment, I noticed her lips were my lips. Her eyes were my eyes. And I hated them. I hated her for giving me her face. I hated my dad for giving me his skin.

For years I struggled with my blackness and my overall identity. Funny thing is you would think as an adult the ridicule, the comparisons, the black shaming would stop. It doesn't. For me, it didn't stop with the dark skin. Now I have to worry about people laughing at my "nappy," "unprofessional" hair. Or wondering why I change my voice over the phone to sound "white." I know that no matter how hard I fight, the thick Redbone will always defeat me. Physically she's more appealing than the "cute for a brown skin girl with the white voice." Ultimately, I have to be OK with that. I have to be OK with that because I have a daughter who will also be that "cute for a little brown skin girl sitting in the corner waiting for life to happen." All because she took after her "momma's side."

What Colorism Did to Me

Chelsea K Brooks

It wasn't until college that I finally believed I was beautiful.

Growing up with a father who never parented me, who hardly ever spoke to me, was enough to make me feel unloved, unwanted.

But to compound this feeling was my chocolate skin.

Except I didn't describe it as chocolate back then.

I described it as dirty. I even despised my father for it. I despised my father for making me this dark, unlovable girl. I needed someone to blame for my lack of beauty.

I felt dirty standing next to white people, next to light skinned black people.

Even today, I have to stop myself from constantly looking over my skin when surrounded by lighter skinned people, and remember that I am beautiful, that my skin is beautiful.

I'm not sure exactly when this all started for me, but I am pretty sure it was the intersection between racism and colorism that lead me to despise my skin.

Being told in the 6th grade that I would be so much prettier if I was lighter really hurt. It hurt even more being told that by a friend.

In 6th grade, I also had a boy ask me to be his girlfriend, out of pity I suspect, because he proceeded to deny that I was his girlfriend to anyone that asked.

He was biracial—Black and Hispanic. He thought I wasn't pretty because I was so dark.

In 8th grade I heard so many "You're so black" jokes I couldn't even keep count.

By high school, I just accepted that I couldn't be pretty because I was so dark.

No matter how many family members, strangers, and family friends told me I was beautiful, that I had beautiful skin, I just couldn't believe it.

When I started mentoring in my senior year of high school, I learned that almost every black girl despised her skin color for one reason or another.

I believe that as a race, black people can tear each other down and be hurtful, spiteful and disrespectful. Part of these actions may come from learned behaviors of past generations of slavery and the times after. It doesn't just happen in the black community—it is just where I have noticed it the most. We may assume that others think they are superior because of their skin color, but we are all really hurting inside for one reason or another.

At some point during my time in college, after many long stares in the mirror, many long nights of reflection, I realized that I am beautiful just the way I am. I learned to thank God for making me as I am. I push other girls and women to feel the same way about themselves. I emphasize to my mentees how beautiful they are in their own skin and explain what I went through. I pass women by in the mall, the grocery store, and try to tell them the same thing. I know it doesn't just happen to dark-skinned Black women. It happens to light skinned women, to Hispanic men and women, to Asian men and women, and to all other ethnicities. It is a problem. But it is one I hope to solve by starting with myself.

I learned to love myself and my skin. I hope that reading my story and the stories of others will inspire someone else to do the same.

Beauty, Like Water

Faith Esene

In a Nigerian city, a woman with skin the color of a praline sprinkles "fair oil" on her face. The product promises to give her a beautiful complexion by making her two times lighter. In another house, a girl dots her palms with Tura skin "toning" cream, or brightening glycerin, to achieve that same goal. Her skin is brown like the bark on the oak trees in her backyard. She wants to blanch her skin so it is the shade of the sticky vanilla ice-cream that drips around her fingers as it melts in the sun. The social sphere has taught them that they should aspire to be "the fairest of them all." Their dark skin is an element of shame. Dark is dull, dirty, undesirable. They want to be like the half-castes who have loose curls that fall about their shoulders and Nigerian skin that has been diluted with a European heritage. Not unique to the African continent—a hemisphere away, a dark Indian woman bleaches her skin to fit a mold created for her.

Yet, the grass is not always greener on the other side of the color divide. Many struggle with self-doubt and shame about their lack of pigmentation, as is the case with those dealing with Albinism or naturally pale skin. In the United States, there is a White woman using a spray tan, or lying in a tanning bed, or soaking up the sun on the warm beach for hours. There is a girl who is rubbing foundation into the folds of her pale skin, foundation that is much too dark for her. Both want to achieve a perky orange glow, even if it is only temporary. They want to avoid looking like ghosts so that the green veins do not jut out on their wrists. They do not want to look like porcelain dolls, with "Oh. Wow! You are so pale!" reverberating on the walls of their social circle.

In another town, a light skinned young man with loose curls is being asked: "So what are you mixed with? You are so handsome."—as if his skin tone is the sole indicator of his beauty, and it could not have come from an unmixed lineage. Though he accepts the compliment, he cannot help but experience a twinge of anxiety at the ostensibly harmless question. Self-doubt creeps in. He wonders if he would still be beautiful if his skin was not this lovely shade of caramel.

*****

The institution of slavery affirmed the color divide. The house slaves were light-complexioned children born of violence. They shouldered lighter tasks to match their fair skin—cooking, child care, clean-up. Dark skinned slaves were given gruesome, filthy tasks to match negative social constructions of blackness. They picked cotton and worms off stalks until their fingers bled. Even after the abolition of slavery, the quality of life often varied based on the mulatto's ability to pass for White. Nonetheless, there is no true difference between house slaves and field slaves because they were both kept in bondage to sustain the economic interest of their owners. So also, there is no difference in the complexions across the color spectrum, because they represent the diversity of the human phenotype and its inherent beauty. Beauty is claustrophobic. Beauty is fluid. As much as each society desires to build standards and boxes around it, it cannot adhere to one confined space because beauty has many different forms. Beauty always manages to seep out of the confines we construct for it.

Colorism—the act of treating one shade of skin as though it is superior to another—attempts to force beauty back into the box. Colorism attempts to grapple with beauty's desire to breathe freely and morph into its various forms. Colorism attempts to scoop up beauty, like water, and throw it back into the box. But beauty slips through the fingers.

Colorism is prevalent in various spheres and bears emotional and psychological effects. In *Nina*, a biographical film about singer Nina Simone, a Dominican woman was cast as the main character, with her face covered in dark make up. Rather than cast someone with a darker complexion, the directors believed that according to western beauty standards a lighter skinned woman—guised albeit haphazardly, to look like Nina Simone—would garner a wider audience. So also, in the film, *Half of a Yellow Sun*, which chronicles the Nigerian Civil War, a biracial actress was cast to play the protagonist Olanna, a young Igbo socialite. However, in the titular novel, Olanna is described as curvy with skin the color of milk chocolate. The actor is given a tan, twists, and a printed dress—instantly transforming her into an authentic Igbo woman. The scenarios in the films mentioned bear connection to the Black Face caricatures of the antebellum era in which White actors painted their faces with charcoal to prepare for Black roles.

If, even in modern society, Black features are relegated to caricatures, what does that say about the Black aesthetic as a whole? Such standards of beauty have resulted in a sense of shame. The psychological ramifications of colorism have been tested in the famous doll studies by Kenneth Clark and in similar subsequent experiments. When researchers asked brown-skinned children to choose which doll they thought was beautiful, most children chose the light-colored or White doll, meaning they identified with a sense of beauty that was outside of themselves—one that would remain elusive.

One solution for combating colorism on a macro level is the spark of a social reconditioning—a realization that outward beauty is transient, thus granting us the freedom to live authentically without trying to twist ourselves into shapes that fit shifting standards. On a micro level, another solution is to give the spectrum of complexions substantial representation in the media—advertising, film, and magazines—and to diversify the cosmetic industry so that society will understand the fluidity of beauty and create opportunities accordingly.

The Color of Water and Me

Abigail Jade Koerner

Looking at me, you might assume I am Latina, Asian, North African, or any other café au lait skin toned ethnic group in the world. My physical appearance is not characteristic of one particular race, but instead represents the looks of many. People I encounter constantly try to claim me. As a little girl on the playground I was blissfully unaware that countless mothers would ask my Mom, "Where did you get her?" These women implied that because my skin was brown and Mom's was white, I could not have come from her. They claimed my race, assuming that since I was living in an area known for a white population, I had to have been adopted from somewhere Brown. Nowadays, these sorts of questions are asked directly of me. Answering is the easy part, I am "white"—my medical records say it, my freckled family members say it— everything except my physical appearance presents me to the outside world as a white person. But looking in the mirror, I recognize that I am not white, and I struggle to find a clear answer as to "what" I am.

As James McBride wrote in his memoir *The Color of Water*, "The question of race was like the power of the moon in my house." Like Mr. McBride, I come from biracial parents; my mom is "white" (of Jewish, Italian, and miscellaneous European heritages) and my dad is probably African-American. Unlike Mr. McBride, who can claim his mother's whiteness and his father's blackness, my father's race is ambiguous. He comes from migrant German parents who, to the best of my knowledge, conceived him, birthed him, and raised him to adulthood. My grandparents were ethnically German and looked the part—my Grandmother has blonde hair and blue eyes and my grandfather was similarly fair. In 1962, my grandmother, grandfather, and their infant daughter (a fellow carrier of recessive genes) arrived in the United States and settled into Mexico, New York, where my father was born five years later. In a picture of my Dad's white family in 1967, there is one clear outlier—my very brown father.

There is no way to know why my Dad came out the way he did. His difference is an unspoken topic as even my father himself denies his brownness. I imagine that as the only non-white member of a rural homogenous community, my Dad noticed that he was different. However, in my 17 years, he has not acknowledged his appearance. This is confusing to me as a Brown person with Brown siblings who all came from the same Brown man. I cannot understand his lack of desire to claim the most visible part of himself.

The question of race may always haunt me, but the question of my origins will not. I come from Washington, DC, the capital of the United States of America. I come from a huge public school where differences make people special. I come from good friends, good food, and a desire to continue to live a good life. Even lacking pieces of the puzzle, I know who I am. Despite these unusual circumstances in my life, I have found a sense of self. I see the advantages to looking the way I do. I think of myself as some kind of chameleon; I blend with whatever group is near. Being unable to identify my race allows me to claim and relate to people of all different colors. I write this essay to claim myself and my soul, though others have tried to claim the color of my skin.

Hues of Hatred and Healing

Janell Lee

Once, when I was younger, just like every other little kid, I was told "sticks and stones may break my bones but words will never hurt me." That's wrong though. Words do hurt. Words can hurt way more than stick and stones ever can. See, sticks and stones can bruise and break you, but you heal after however long. Words, though? Words stick around much longer than any bruise. They are wounds that dig under the skin and find a nook or corner to lodge themselves that don't bother you until something draws them out, whether it be intentional or not. Wounds that become part of us in moments of weakness, something anyone can experience.

There are words, though, that hurt more than others. Particularly ones that aim to target something that cannot be changed, like skin colour. In today's society, these words fly around like magpies, darting in and out of the air, attacking with random or unseen hatred. They peck and punch and scar over, resulting in traumatic memories. The worst part is, it doesn't stop. As long as there is ignorance and hatred and misinformation spread everywhere. Wounds like those don't fade after 4 or 5 years, they remain in the heart, where every word winds its way in. They define you in the moment and you think "what am I worth? Is this all I am?"

Such things can circle and spread like wildfire. There is colourism in everyday life, a byproduct or child, if you will, of racism. It is target-to-target oppression. It is the discrimination of others, made by those who rule and perpetuated by those who themselves feel oppressed. Call it a Russian doll of discrimination. The hues of skin, the feel of hair, the colour of eyes aren't things that should define anyone, much less confine anyone. Features that cannot be changed, like birthmarks, are what make us into who we are. To attack those things is to attack who someone is as a person. Those that bully, the ones who place hatred upon minorities, speak clearly through their actions: "If I am being made fun of, if I am not good enough, then neither are you. If I cannot live peacefully, no one shall."

This mentality must be stopped, the throwing of words like verbal sticks and stones is not just a child's rhyme anymore. It is more than that, it has always been more than that. As long as hatred, ignorance, and falsity are spread, wounds caused by words will continue to fester, never truly healing. There are just too many who are too blind to see it and stop it. We all stop singing nursery rhymes at a certain point in our lives, the age where we are introduced into the real world and told "no, words can hurt you, often more than weapons can." So many have to wonder when or if they will be hit with such weapons, the ones that leave no visible marks, and if they do, how true they are. We must show anyone who has been teased, bullied, and marked as less than for things they cannot and should not have to feel bad about or change, that they are perfect. Today is the day to offer a hand to help lift up those who've been put down, and offer words that caress and care rather than beat and bruise. Today starts as the day where nursery rhymes are left in the past, in childhood memories, in a time where that is all they are.

Black by Nature

Stella Mpisi

I cried myself to sleep. In the morning, when I looked in the mirror before school, I hated what I saw. I pulled the skin at the corners of my eyes to make them look smaller; I pinched my nose as tightly as I could to make it look less flat; I laid my hands flat on my hair to make it look sleek; and with rage, I scrubbed my face with a luffa, hoping that my skin would look lighter… but none of this worked, and so at night I cried myself to sleep.

Nine years old. I was only nine years old when a group of black kids at school started calling me "black by nature." The nickname quickly caught on, and many more kids soon found it amusing to call me by the name they deemed suitable to describe my dark skin. I didn't understand that it was discrimination; instead, I unconsciously believed that there was indeed something wrong with my dark skin. The nine-year-old in me struggled to comprehend why I had to look the way I did while my peers had skin, hair, and noses which were "acceptable." Why had Mother Nature deprived me of my mother's long hair and fair skin? I didn't have answers to my questions and my self-esteem soon died. Every time I walked past a group of kids who yelled "here comes black by nature!" I ducked my head in shame and fought to hide back my tears. I was only nine years old.

Acceptable. What made lighter skin acceptable? Why did the boys at school laugh at me while they praised the light-skinned biracial girls? Why did the light-skinned girls mock me and tell me to stay out of the sun otherwise I would "become darker"? When I reached high school and had my first "real" crush on a boy, I envied the girls who had fair skin. They got all the attention, whilst none of the boys seemed to even notice me. At fifteen years old, I tried to chemically lighten my skin for the first time. The instructions on the box of the bar of soap I had bought with my hard-earned money told me to wash the soap off my face after two minutes; I, however, left it on for ten minutes even though I could feel it burn. I wanted to be liked and I wanted my skin to be acceptable; instead I burnt my skin, and my classmates laughed at my obvious failed skin bleaching attempt. Why wasn't my skin acceptable?

Melanin. As I eased into adulthood, I realized that it didn't make any sense to be judged solely based on the quantity of melanin in my skin. Although I realized that my childhood memories were those of discrimination and low self-esteem, I still felt like there was something wrong with me. I understood the concept of melanin, but I didn't understand why Mother Nature had given me so much of it. Why did my abundant melanin place me at the bottom of the social hierarchy? Even though I was no longer a child, I still felt intimidated by lighter-skinned women. After years of being told that I was ugly and "too dark," it was difficult to remove the shackles of a complex of inferiority that ran so deep it had become a part of me. On the surface, I told myself that my skin tone did not define me, but deep down I continued to resent it and to envy my peers who had less melanin.

Colorism. From the young age of nine years old, a cloud of discrimination constantly hung above my head and I cried myself to sleep. I was alienated by my peers simply because of the color of my skin. I was unconsciously led to believe that lighter skin was more acceptable. But what is acceptable skin? What amount of melanin does one need in order to be deemed acceptable? ... Mother Nature made me who I am; and today, a nickname which once planted a seed of anger and self-hate deep inside me is now a name I recognize as a truth that makes me the strong, intelligent, and beautiful black woman that I am. I am Black by Nature. I am me.

Black Tea

Edoka Writes

At nine years-old, my white, antique vanity was my first love. I'd stare and pose into the three-way mirror, as though channeling the future of social media. With tiny hands, I'd stretch my curls, searching for the perfect profile. And when satisfaction seemed too distant, I'd improvise. My father's beige t-shirts worked well for the long, light colored hair I desired. And from the pretend cosmetics set I'd request every birthday, Barbie pink lipstick was the solution to brightening my tan skin.

But Barbie wasn't the beauty I was striving to reflect. It was my mother. A Louisiana Creole with silky auburn hair and forest green eyes with a fiery tangerine circle that hugged her pupils. My mother's personality matched those eyes, but her features were less telling.

Her long nose widened toward the tip. Her lips average in size but uniquely tinted—pinkish with a subtle hint of brown, perhaps from cigarette smoking. Today, her physique might be considered blah, but back then it was bam; think Suzanne Somers. And when she'd enter a room commotion commenced. I learned quickly from the adults of color around me, be it strangers or family, that her appearance was worthy of praise. I was proud to call her mom.

Born and raised in New Orleans, I was brought up in a predominately Creole neighborhood. For me, that meant little contact with whites and moderate contact with blacks. That said, the community embraced the latter, with the exception of certain families who shunned marital intermingling. After all, why would a good-looking Creole marry a black and risk a nappy haired child?

But changes occur in life and we begin to see our world differently. My epiphany began in high school, at which point my family resided elsewhere and neighborhoods were more inclusive. The school I attended was largely African-American. My first week of 9th grade was a blazing hell, yet a slow dripping cloud began to save me from the ever-present self-loathing.

Girls will be girls—good or bad. The hallway sneers were worse than getting my hair taped, because behind the sneers I saw evil. The verbal assaults happened at any given moment, but it wasn't the words that hurt; it was the hatred stemming from the insults. I began to skip school and smoke marijuana. I started sneaking my dad's alcohol into hairspray bottles, downing it before class. But one day, when clarity stepped in by the name of Letitia Davis, my mind took a turn for the better.

"Hey, what's your name?" she asked.

It's Bridget.

"I see you at school," she said. "I see how those girl's treat you. Fuck them. I'm not jealous of you. Not everybody wants a light-skinned girl. I get dudes, too. They love this pretty brown skin. Shit! I'll be your friend," giggled Letitia.

My smile spread deeper than my wounds. Peace was upon me. And that cloud dripping over my head burst, baptizing me with new life.

My days were easier, though the battle continued. The attempts to jump and trip me remained until graduation day. Looking back, I feel sorrow for the teen girls and their self-projected inadequacy. I understand where that horrid venom might have rooted. In a nutshell, color preference or lack thereof exists because attention and value are given to one color over the other.

But there's a rainbow of African-Americans out here. And individuals with insecurities and prejudices must realize that we as a people, were dismembered because of how we look. And the energy used to insult and divide further can easily transfer into self-love, which elicits an organic beauty seen beyond any complexion.

POEMS

My Skin is Not My Sin

Arigo Dut

Age: 11
Location: Canada

Cold eyed and soulless,
A little kid—just like me—calls me a Nigger. His name still
etched in my memory, undeserving of my voice he shall
remain nameless.
Only four years in this foreign land and my ears knew that
this word was not to be heard nor received. I knew, at
the age of 11, once it rippled in the air and made its way
into your being it could destroy your every...being.

The images of ROOTS flashed before me and I knew
what I had to do.
Mama told me this is a story you must see. This is a story
you must know. This is the story of our people.
This is my story. This is your story.

I walk, defeated but not broken, and knock on the solid
door of my Vice Principal's office. The mahogany deep
brown door is like my skin, but I do not possess the
strength of its roots.
"Susan," what's wrong? Foreign land, foreign name.
What has become of me?
He senses my silence, my defeat, the absence of me.
I say, quietly, "He who shall remain nameless called me the
'N' word."

Sweet man. His eyes tell me he can't even fathom what
that word means...
I whisper as if I was the one who just attempted to destroy
a being with my words: "Nigger." Shocked and eyes
filled with intent, he does what I could not—takes a
stand.

Age: 11
Location: Canada

Slowly regaining my strength, I turn the corner.
Cold eyed and soulless. A little kid—just like me—calls me
a Nigger...
once more.

My skin is NOT my sin.
My skin is my strength.
My skin is sacred.

Age: 19
Location: Mexico

The sun picks up the myriad hues of my skin. The dark,
mahogany browns, the golden, honey coloured
undertones, the black, ebony shield passed down to me
by my Ancestors. Desperately wanting to take in and
absorb every ray I can because my other home does not
always afford me this "privilege," I go to the pool.
While my soul sister—the Eritrean Goddess smudged in
the smoke of her Aboriginal Ancestors, My Canadian
beauty, laced together with multiple Nordic and
European bloodlines—remains in the hotel room.

After completely soaking myself, allowing myself to be
   consumed by Mother Nature's wetness. The blue ocean
   waters bring me back to life because I knew, at the age
   of 19, Water is Life.

I wait patiently in line to return my towel. A young girl—
   just like me—stares at me. Her eyes not cold or
   soulless...but empty. She comes towards me... I stay
   still, trying to speak to her but unable too.
We are both the various colours of roasted almonds.
   Children of the same blood trail, but we do not
   understand one another. Wanting to help, I motion to
   the towel line because the heart of my Ancestors always
   offers a helping hand... She begins to touch me without
   my consent
Rubbing me as if I am nothing but an attraction, an
   animal.
She calls her boyfriend to come touch my skin.
Shocked and bewildered, he knew that for some people I
   am nothing more than my skin...

My skin is NOT my sin.
My skin is my sultriness.
My skin is sacred.

Age: 22
Location: United States of America

Rocking and strutting in my white two-piece bikini, I am
   whole as I walk down the poolside. The Vegas heat is
   dangerous; it can make you easily sin.
I walk pass a Black male, his hues filtered down through
   generations
He looks at me in awe as I pass.

I hear him say: "She is gorgeous."
Salted and seated in the shady underpinnings of an
     umbrella. Two women, Black women, their hues
     filtered through generations, look at me with disgust
     and say: "She is so dark." I knew, at the age of 22, that
     these words were not their own.

My skin is NOT my sin.
My skin is my sweetness.
My skin is sacred.

Age: 24
Location Egypt:

Temporarily on the "cognitive" tip of the Motherland.
     Falsely believing I was back home. Foolishly thinking I
     would be as safe as I was in the arms of my Mother. My
     cousins—two South Sudanese Goddesses who
     exemplify the richness of pure unfiltered beauty—and I
     walk into the hustle, bustle streets of an African market.

A woman drenched in darkness, clothed in black from the
     top of her head to the bottom of her feet, only has a
     slight opening for her eyes. Her bright blue eyes give
     the false impression of light...goodness. She throws a
     sharp, ragged rock at us...
I'm not sure what made me stop...hesitate. Maybe it was
     my Guardian Angles: My Baba, My sister.
Who each grabbed my feet and held them down.
Who each prevented me from being struck or being
     broken.

She hits another Egyptian man, one of her own. She says, "Malaish," to the man; Not to the three girls who she tried to strike down. Our colourful clothes, bright smiles, blinding light. I knew, at age 24, that our skin was too much for her to witness.

My skin is NOT my sin.
My skin is my sacrifice.
My skin is sacred.

Your skin is Not my sin.
    Your skin is sacred.

I Grew Up Hating Myself

Katrielle Ely Francke

I was three when it hit me
That I was not beautiful.
When my little brother was born
His skin was pale and smooth—
What I wished mine to be.
There sat my grandmother
Looking at the perfection of his skin
While I stared down at my own sunburnt brown
Matching my father's darker tone
Rather than the mixed lights of my mother

It was when I was told by my family
Ways to lighten my skin
With orange peels and lotions
And to always carry around an umbrella
And hide from the sun.
There came pictures of cousins—
The mestizos
Prized for their fair skin
Their stick-straight hair
And the idea that beauty was something to work towards

It was during a class lesson on Filipino natives
That I'd compare myself to every classmate I had
Did I look mestizo enough?
Which were negritos and which weren't?
I was content
With the little Chinese in my blood

Because it resulted in a lighter brown
Than the natives of my own country
Of which I take pride in
But only as part of the lighter population.

I was at the age of seven when we moved
And I saw that the U.S. was diverse
Pigmentation ranging from fair to dark
And I was jealous of those with a lighter complexion
Who envied my skin
That tanned easily under the sun
And I wondered
Why would they want
To risk their light shade
And burn their perfect hue?

It was at the age of 13 when we went back
And I was still not beautiful
And I envied the stick straight
Chemically treated hair I saw
And I compared my face
To the Intsik
With their smaller, paler image
And so I straightened my straight hair
And bought face cleanser that stung
To try being more beautiful

It was at the age of 15 when I despised
And hated who I was
And where I came from
And asked myself:
Why can't I have fair skin, nice hair,
And a nose that didn't take up half my face?
Here came the face massages and makeup

Shades lighter than my own
Here came the mask created
To hide my insecurities

It was a few months back that I realized
That the subliminal messages I received
Of how lighter is better
And straight hair is ideal
How a flat nose is not beautiful
Were standards that I could never achieve
And were never meant to break me
But there was no way to ignore those words
Although beauty changes
The damage is done

I'm older now
And I am still not beautiful
With my tan complexion
And hair darker than night
And face flat and wide
And self-hatred that made me ugly
I am not beautiful
And I will admit that I'm not
I will not continue to define myself
By a false idea of beauty

A Diamond Broken Free

Sharon Harrison

Complexion like a chocolate bar
Smooth as silk
Always put down as a child for having
A darker complexion, hiding the insecurities
On the inside smiling bright as the sun
On the Outside letting the mean comments roll off
Like a waterfall
Questioning why I'm I different from the rest

A diamond in the rough trying to break free
My shade is beautiful in every light
The darker the berry
The sweeter the juice
I agree
My shine is finally breaking free
Refusing to believe I'm only beautiful for a dark skin girl
I'm beautiful because God made me
I'm a diamond
Finally broken free

Loving me in every way
The darkness of my skin
The sparkle of my eyes and
The mold of my body
Everything from God shining bright as a diamond
Being sweet as a berry
Yes, I am
A dark skin girl

Finding My Place

Anastasia Hirschi

Sometimes my dark skin
burns darker with humiliation.
Sometimes my dark eyes
burn darker with shame.
Where can someone go
In a place they don't belong?

Walking down the hallways,
Everybody turns.
Everybody glances.
They might think—
I can't see her.

But I know they do.

Sometimes it hurts.
I wish I had a rock to throw
To watch it skip
over and over
because that's how it feels.

I want to fit in sometimes,
To be like the rest.
I remember our differences
and why it can never be
I watch them walk away without me.

All around me

I see pictures
of perfect people
with perfect hair and skin.
Can that ever be me—with my hair and skin?

All at once—
I don't know when it happened—
I realize no matter what color my skin is,
I will find my place in the world.
I am my own beautiful.

And I know that I am.

Colorism

Anam Hussain

You see my color,
Dark like night,
Dark like grey smoke.
You see my face,
Think so low.
It's such a disgrace
Your mind is too weak
To see beauty
That lies beneath
This hue of sweet,
Sweet like chocolate,
Pure and real.
What you see is true.
No two faces you'll see.
My shade is nothing more than a blessing.
Not my fault if your eyes are scratched,
Not able to see.
Humanity is clear
No color is anywhere near
You must be lost, no love in your life.
Wonder why
You loathe my color
To cover and to disguise.
All you do,
I will not mind.
My color makes me stronger,
More than your mind.
Remember one thing:

Stars shine up high,
But they cannot shine
Without the dark tint in the sky.

The Skin I'm In

Abena Johnson

My skin, my skin
Oh, how I love my skin
So beautiful, so rich
And so black.
My skin, my skin
Oh, how I love my skin
So different, so powerful
My skin could never make me cowardful.
My skin, my skin
Oh, how I love my skin
A reminder of my motherland
A reminder of the ones before me who held the same
    color of my hand.
My skin, my skin
Oh, how I love my skin
It might have started wars
But it can open up doors
And remind me of what I'm fighting for.
This is my skin, my skin!
And oh, how I love my skin
The skin that I'm so beautiful in!

Untitled

Aaliyah J.

That boy. Every Black girl knows at least a dozen of those boys. The kind of boys who only date the "racially ambiguous" girls. The kind of girls inhabiting skin that makes everyone ask, "What are you?" I guess I'm one of those girls, but it depends on who you ask. In my white classroom full of White and White-adjacent faces, we had a substitute teacher, a dark skinned Black woman. My friend and I, the only Black girls, sit next to each other and chat in between our work. My voice must have turned into a bullhorn so subtly I didn't even notice, because here I am being hushed. Never mind all of the other voices; mine was the one ringing out when I wasn't aware I was even using it. She calls me to her desk. She tells me that with all that talking I'm doing there's no way I was getting my work done. I'm a parade of "ma'am"s and "I'm sorry"s and polite silence, even as she cuts me off twice mid-sentence. My work was done. My friend and I finished before everyone else. This is a group assignment, anyway, so we are allowed to talk. My smile must have had "bad intentions" smeared across it; she didn't smile back. I return to my desk. I'm vaguely annoyed and not at all surprised when the substitute makes her way across the room, stopping near my desk to survey my assignment, hushing none of the faces that looked nothing like mine. On her next rotation around, she stops at my friend's desk. My friend is five feet, with eight inches of long, honey-colored, curly hair. The only thing chocolate about that girl is her beautiful eyes, and of course the teacher made a point to tell her about it. She gushed over how beautiful she was, how gorgeous her skin was, how amazing her hair was. Everything started to fall in place. Of course I couldn't prove why the teacher showed favoritism to everyone but me, but there's no doubt in a Black girl's stomach about whether or not she's being discriminated against. It's a blessing and a curse. I tried telling my friend what I thought was going on, but she didn't get it. And why would she attempt to understand when doing so would make her just another nigga?

Prophecy

aisha khan

she awoke with the desire
to slaughter the heritage
that nested within her
a conflict that bloomed
with every glance at a mirror;
her skin had been deemed
a shade too drab for the night,
yet a tint too pale for the
moon.
thus, she clutched onto
the stars that lingered,
until they no longer did;
for they too had realized
that she was merely an ugly
conundrum.
light skin, dark soul—
she was slowly vanishing
within the folds of the
phenomenon
that was her complex
complexion.
she had come to memorize the
names that scraped her skin:
skunk, caramel, halfro
but the one she held dearest
could not escape
her lips.
too white to be black

too black to be white
where was the line?
perhaps she was the line;
the perfect inequality of
grime and gale
frost and flare
—though where she was drawn,
she knew not.
but in that ambiguity
she found beauty—
for her skin spoke louder
than she.
it inhabited scars
of a half that
bled, ached, grieved still
and bore them proudly.
a chameleon tethered to
two pickets,
she never could tear
away from one
without marring the
other.
but she need not
tear away, for
escaping herself
would harm,
embracing herself
would heal.

The Life of a Nutty Buddy

Lillian G. Lewis

Life as a kid was strange when I look back at it.
It was strange that I would get compliments a lot,
But my cousin wouldn't.
I thought we looked just alike—
Melanin filled skin, kinky hair and a big nose—
But I guess I was wrong,
Because while I got complimented for my copper
    corkscrew curls,
She was told to get weave.
When I was praised for my caramel colored, sun kissed
    skin,
She was told to go inside, that she was already dark
    enough.

We were 6.

Funny thing is, I wanted to look just like her and my
    aunt—
Big curves, dark skin, and hair that looked like a crown.
She looked like a Fudge Pop, and I was just the plain, tan
    stick that held it up.
I never thought about how she might have wanted to trade
    places too.
I thought maybe if I was a few shades darker
People wouldn't ask about my parents;
They wouldn't ask which one of them was the vanilla ice
    cream and who was the chocolate coating.
That made me, a Nutty Buddy.

I wanted to be one shade so badly; I didn't want to be
      stuck in between this bi-
            racial limbo.
I was too white for the black kids and too black for the
      white kids.
I was told not to embrace who I am,
To either inject myself with more stereotypes or kick all
      the melanin out of my
       skin and leave it
on the curb like an old couch.
And that's exactly what I did.
For the first time, I rejected who I really am
And oh, how it tasted bittersweet.

I was 7.

I took moving schools as a golden opportunity to officially
      write my skin a final
            Dear John letter.
It just wasn't working out between the two of us, so I
      wanted to call it quits.
Although my skin objected, my heart overpowered it, and
      from that day on I filled
            myself to the brim with stereotypes and self-hatred,
But my skin was a permanent reminder that no matter
      what
I would still be stuck between two very different worlds
Two worlds that would never accept me
Two worlds that would always send me back to the other
      side like an endless game of
            Red Rover
"Red Rover, Red Rover send that bi-racial girl over!"
And back and forth I ran
Until I decided that I wanted to stay on the lighter side

After all you can only run but so much.

I was 9.

After I started to look more like a Fudge Pop myself, I
    wanted to turn back into a
        stick.
My hair was starting to grow into a crown like shape too.
My nose was still squished in and took up half of my face,
    and my body began to
        get those big curves I had wanted all my life.
But suddenly, when I got them, I didn't want them
    anymore.
And all I wanted was to be as white as snow and look like
    those girls on TV;
Their noses looked like buttons and their eyes were
    spectacular colors—unlike
        Mine.
They had beautiful, rectilinear, light-colored locks, while
    mine were the color of rust and
        looked like curly fries.
I felt rejected by the world, but surprisingly,
I never straightened my curls
Or bleached my hair
Or tried to lighten my skin because deep down
I think I knew that I was as beautiful as those girls on TV
Even if I didn't know it yet.

I was 13.

Eventually I realized black was not a synonym for bad;
I remember when I realized this too:
It was Social Studies class during my last year of Junior
    High.

For once I was really learning about the darker side of me,
How much some of my ancestors truly endured
And how some of them benefited from this rigged system.
I finally learned that everything was not perfect after the
	Emancipation
			Proclamation
I learned that Martin Luther King was murdered, he didn't
	just die.
I learned about the Black Panther Party and how they were
	labeled as a terrorist
			group but the KKK was allowed to walk free.
I finally learned that even today, the system is still rigged
	for me
And my Dad
And my Aunt
And my Grandma
And my cousin—
 whom for so long I wanted to be just like.
But now I can finally stop playing that game of Red Rover
Because whether anyone likes it or not,
I can be both, and I am.

No longer will I force feed myself lies and hatred,
No longer will I deny who I really am—
A little mixed girl,
One with the insane dream of being a writer,
And one who will never deny who she is anymore.
No longer will I force myself to choose one side, and
	anyone that tries to get me
		to choose will be tossed aside like old leftovers.

I won't say that everything magically changed for me,
	though.
I'm taking baby steps,

Just like they did.

I wonder what my ancestors would say now if they could
see me.

Did they ever think that a love between two different races
was possible? Or would they push me aside as well,

Treating me as if I'm a freak of nature?

I guess I'll never know.

But each day I'm getting better and better

And each day I realize more and more

Maybe it's not so bad being a Nutty Buddy after all....

Her Every Feature, Except Her Skin

LSimoneM

she rejects any man who looks like her—
dark
light skin will give her light babies
maybe
she doesn't want her children to be
hated
berated
humiliated
'cause of their dark outer covering
protecting her children from verbal abusers is good
    mothering
the inside matters, yet the outside is what's seen
the torture and degradation that dark skin brings
she doesn't want her children to feel what she lived
it didn't matter how smart and talented she was,
and how much of her kindness she would give
her dark skin kept her chained in a corner
and she wasn't alone
she was with every other dark girl
who was laughed and pointed at in the world
called monkey, ugly, burnt and black as the ace of spades
the memories of name calling and rejection that would
    never fade
a husband, who has light skin, will change her life
if only he wants her as his wife
her children can have her every feature, except her skin

light skin her choice of hue
intelligent, beautiful, talented, dark-skinned woman,
his light skin is no guarantee; you must consider the entire
    pedigree
your dark skin and his light skin may produce children
    darker than you
then what are you gonna do?
teach them about what you didn't have
self-love, not light skin
treat them how you were not
compliment the skin they're in

Melanin

Shamiika Mitchell

Melanin is the beauty of my skin, the riches deep within
The beauty of my descendants, the faith that builds my
strength
Barriers that have been broken within, my melanin is
courageous, easily to offend
My skin is beautiful. Black as coal, paper sack brown,
honey gold, lightly tan, bronze, almond sand, cocoa
with a touch of cream
My melanin explodes my self-esteem. My melanin means
Queen
Promised dreams, riches unforeseen
My melanin is fear and faith.
If black is bad, and melanin is last,
Then who must be first? You were the first to steal from
the melanin on this earth.
So, what is it we're truly worth? Black cannot mean bad or
cursed
Putting a price tag on my melanin would never hurt. The
rays from the sun disbursed, enriches the color of my
skin. Deeply rooted outside and within
Melanin, melanin, they lay under laser lights just for you
Pay thousands of dollars to feel you. Or should I say, *me*?
Laughing hysterically my melanin is free. All my sisters
wear it gracefully
Sitting back, calm, hundreds of years, watching your fears
Jealously, ignorant ways in your secret closet, begging God
for melanin traits

My melanin is often despised, discredited, mocked publicly
     abused
Straight, curly, kinky hair matched well with my melanin
     100% approved
No more denying pigmentations of my skin
Flawless, phenomenal, highly favored and blessed
Over 500 years you assumed we were oppressed, stressed,
     worth less
Melanin sisters we passed society's test, perfecting our
     melanin to display at its best

What We Fear

Pauline Monter

I grew up being taught by the society in my country
that dark didn't mean beautiful.
In a place populated by people
whose pigments bear the mark of the earth,
I was taught to stay indoors
for fear of being burned by the sun's affection.

There's a stigma against dark skin in my homeland.
See, dark is a mark of poverty.
Lack of education.
Your shell is an aberration from european beauty
    standards,
as if born a mutation,
unwelcomed in your own nation,
but you learn that colorism is an effect of colonization,
made worse by globalization

Can you imagine living in a city where every other
    billboard is a notion
of underlying persuasion hinting that whitening your skin
    is the better choice?

They taught us that black was dirty because god was light
that there was only one type of beauty:
white.

I grew up surrounded by people recklessly saying,
"She would be so pretty if she wasn't morena,"

and mothers yelling at their daughters to hurry up and
     come home so they don't get dark
as if the night could swallow us up and inject black blood
     in our veins
to turn us into creatures of old myths and folklore,

nobody wanted to be an aswang, not a manananggal,
especially not a "negrito."

We feared the dark because we could not make sense of it
and so we made it embody evil,
and it never made sense, but we believed them.

See, I lived for seven years hiding in the shade because I
     was told
I could fall like Icarus did,
even when my feet were rooted to the ground,
the sky could swallow me up any minute
and turn my wax wings liquid.

And I was afraid of the repercussions of being different,
because I saw the decay of those with brown skin on the
     pavement.
And I thought that by coming to the land of the free,
I'd be able to escape watching children dance with death
     on our sidewalks
but it seems our civil servants hold hunger like a trophy in
     their hands,
pull the trigger, and it's the same scene all over again.

Subbi

Subbi Namakula

Out in the countryside of Kayindu, Uganda
Under my grandmother's mango tree,
I feel my mother's warm breath on my neck.

She weaves her legacy into my scalp,
Pulling and twisting my hair into yarn.
Her red fingernails, sting my head.

She coils threads of yarn in my hair,
pulling until my face contorts in pain.
My mother's fingers speak the language of
generations of African mothers.
Warm tears fall down my cheeks.
She hums and sings:

Subbi, Subbi, Subbi, mwana wange
tonamera berre
lwolimera berre
Lwedigenda naye.

Her voice roots itself in strands of my hair,
attaches fibers of Ugandan Myths and poems,
Maroon Sunrises,
Songs of birds under mango trees.

My mother spins self-love
and gratitude and wonder
into strands of twisted yarn on my head.

We both know
This will be the last time
I feel her fingers comb through my dark hair
I feel her sweet papaya breath on my neck
this will be the last time I hear her call me "Subbi."

Before I fly 8000 miles
into a Chicago January
where everything is white,
where shivering Subbi also becomes whitened
and is now called "Charlotte."

Her stepmother untwists Ugandan braids,
And for four hours,
strands of her mother's legacy
attached to black yarn
fall
on the pink tiles of the bathroom.
Her stepmother slathers on relaxers
to destroy the curls and coils of her hair;
They kill the ebizikkes and sebuttos
And silence the song birds.
The scent of mango and papaya is washed away by Dark &
    Lovely.
Relaxers, Relaxers, RELAX.
but Charlotte cannot relax.

Because her skin is too dark and could never be fair &
    lovely.
After school on Monday,
through the snow of Racine and 78th street,
Charlotte shamefully walks to Walgreens
then hides in her step-mother's bathroom

and rubs bleach on her skin.

Subbi, Subbi, Subbi, mwana wange
tonamera berre
lwolimera berre
Lwedigenda nawe.

White Asia

Sabrina M. Pyun

Unfortunately, I must admit
I am so naturally that Asian
scheme of beauty:

Skin translucent as steamed rice,
"paler than the moon"—what Ling wants
in Mulan. I am the daughter my mother calls
"pretty white face," while my little
sister is brown as a jackrabbit.
I am the girlfriend whose boyfriend
can't help but admire the milkiness
of her snowy curves.

And what's not to love
but the fact that I am the face
of a worldwide marketing campaign
to scrub the blackness out of Asia?

I am pale billboard girls advertising
those euphemistic "brightening" masks.
I am the DIY citric acid facial scrub
a brown girl grinds into her face.
I am the 3 shades of peachy foundation
Etude House offers: beige, fair, and sand.

My paleness is a politicized commodity.
It is the root of East Asian Imperialism
and the cause of the Japanese occupation

of Korea and the Nanjing Massacre:
The race to be the whitest Asian country
in order to appeal to its European counterparts.

It is why today, Japanese girls use umbrellas on sunny days,
why Korean beauty products are unparalleled,
and why Asia clings to its mismatched foundation.

So aren't I lucky
I am the standard?
And shouldn't I be honored
that millions of girls want to look like me?

Well, I went to Korea
and I was admired.

How hollow a feeling it is.

My Brother

Gladis Isabel Ricaurte

Wide burgeoning nose bridges,
connecting our homologous eyes,
stapling our identity—
alike taxonomy,
yet different shades.
"Are you dating?"
"That's my brother."
"He's so dark."
"He is my brother."
Homologous features
Polar shades,
Seemingly altering every feature.
Resemblant curvatures are now classified as European and
    African.
Bridges we share to connect are now the bridges that
    detach us.
I share the similar taxonomy with that mammal.
Geographically, we were born in the same place.
Racial divisions are quizzically berated among us—
Since we are one.
Passionate Latin orators have told us we are one,
so why is it in America that he is more African and I am
    more European?
Acknowledge the taxonomy;
Do not acknowledge the enmeshed American social
    constructions that come with it.
It is evolution and genetics
not a signal for eugenics.

Humanity does not need eugenics.

· Humanity is already pure, and taxonomizing it should not elicit inferiority.

Scan for more suicide awareness and information

From Mental Health and Wellness Committee

I Am More

Krithika Shrinivas

I am brown, and my own culture tells me that having light
skin and eyes are the only way for me to be loved.

I am brown, streaked in melanin and dotted with furry
body hair.

I am brown, and I learned at a young age that the lessons
on equality in grade school were only a safety blanket
against the real world.

I am brown, and I never wanted to be. My cocoa skin and
raven hair is frowned upon, the unwanted mien of a
white-washed nation.

I am brown, and my motherland shuns me. Merry, light
girls are admired; their pupils are studded emeralds and
their pale skin scintillates.

I am brown, and I am aware of it with every visit to my
native land. Advertisements feature models wearing
caked powder—their clear skin putting me to shame.

I am brown, and my classmates eye me in scorn,
suggesting scrubs and bleach creams to rid me of the
tone I was born with.

I am brown, and I tell myself that I can change—be light, pretty—if I just wear sweaters, drink fruit juice and scrub my body with citrus.

I am brown, but cut through my skin, and I'll burst of stars and hope. My heart holds wisps of dreams that you can lace through your hands, and my veins will bleed of crimson love.

I am brown, and I am more than this layer that drapes my body.

A Legacy of Colorism

Elizabeth Upshur

I wish my mother was less laissez-faire about color.
My identity was a playground insult.
My village was bone white,
no soul sisters, no brothas.
My grown up self fires back,
wraps that hurt up,
labels that incident
under things marked "duh" and "of course."
I am a Transatlantic joke, with the punchline:
388,000 Middle Passage survivors
explode like wild oats in spring
400 years, slave, and Freeman to be my ancestors
counted as chattel in the census

1528, Spain's Florida. Karankawa, the Chief, wet his
    thumb,
slid it across the African slave Esteban's cheek
and marveled at his unstained digit.

my maternal ancestor—Ghana black,
all slave in Orangeburg, South Carolina.
my paternal ancestor—straight up white in Richmond,
    Virginia.
Then Pennsylvanian, all the way down to paternal
    grandparents—paper bag black.
And me—brown skinned, in between.

cut to now,
cut to blue vein
Black girls wash out
their color with bleach
like blood of Jehovah
water skin with cocoa
butter and jojoba
No one fucks with dark girls
So lighten up
let the white girls tan.

Growing up in the suburban South,
my sisters and I, we whispered, worried
about my father, who had blue
eyes but our kinky hair. My sisters
asked, "Mom is dad Black?"
My older sister Kyra held up
her arm for evidence;
she said he was a lot lighter
a lot paler than some white people.
He's black and light, mom
sighed, diced onions for chili.
She never said how black
people got so light.

"If you light, you alright!"
boys repeat
what was thrown at us
by enslavers in words, whips
with pale-grabbing-holding-down
-taking-who-they-wanted hands.
That is how we got so light. Became one
drop Black, but a few drops

white enough to be mistaken
for Latina, light skin, pretty girl.

Brown Skin Jawn

Tajinnea Wilson

I used to be so thankful
that I wasn't a light skin chick
or a dark skin girl
I was content
with being a brown skin jawn

it meant I wasn't foreign
or badd as shit
but it also meant I wasn't a burnt piece of toast
I was a bit better or good enough
like one step above a bronze medal

"Mr. Burrell, If the dark skin slaves have to work in the field
and the light skin slaves work in the house, then
where do the brown skin slaves work?"

"Probably on the porch?"

"Somewhere in the shade, so we don't get darker!"

I have just the right amount of melanin, thank god
brown skin jawns don't curve you
at least not as often as those light skin one's do
and don't always have an attitude problem
not like them mean ass dark skins

I never added #TeamBrownSkin to my twitter bio
but I do like it when snapchat filters
make me look lighter
and add blush to my cheeks

the boys still can't decide
if I'm brown sugar or caramel
but I don't want to be either
I'd rather be thought provoking
I'm no longer content
with being a brown skin jawn

her amount of melanin makes her more valuable
more desirable than me?
and my melanin makes me one step above the next black queen?

that's dead
the whole idea is trash
and we know it is
always have

About the Authors

Ebonie Adams
Ebonie is a lifelong native of Stamford, CT where she lives with her husband and daughter. She has always had a passion for writing and the arts, but was afraid to showcase her talent. She decided that 2017 would be her year to "Jump."

Chelsea K Brooks
Chelsea is a recent Master of Social Work grad from the University of Georgia. Along with her current job in foster care, writing and performing poetry are her passions. Through writing, she aims to inspire and give voices to those who go unheard.

Arigo Dut
Arigo Dut is a new addition to the art scene in Edmonton, Alberta, Canada. Born in South Sudan and raised in Edmonton, Arigo brings a unique multi-layered voice to her poetry. Arigo Dut graduated from MacEwan University and has a Bachelor's in Communication Studies. She is the founder of Dut Designs, a full-scale communications service.

Faith Esene
Faith Esene is a Nigerian-American undergraduate writer from Maryland. When she is not writing, she can be found engaging in critical conversations. Her work has been featured in *Sterling Notes*, and the anthology, *Love Letters to Our Daughters*.

Katrielle Ely Francke

Katrielle Ely Francke is a recent high school graduate, and will be continuing her education at Arizona State University. This is the first of her works to be published. She hopes that her poem, although fueled by bitterness, could help heal others.

Sharon Harrison

Sharon is a dark skin girl. She was put down for her skin tone a lot as a child. However, it taught her to love herself no matter what. She is a strong, caring, and loving person.

Anastasia Hirschi

Anastasia is a romantic. She has enjoyed reading, writing poetry, and romance novels since she was in junior high. She enjoys music and the arts. She is currently an English major at Brigham Young University (BYU).

Anam Hussain

She is currently in High-school. She enjoys reading and writing, especially poems. Anam also loves to go on adventures, travel, and she also has a passion for photography. Her main goal in life is to live life to the fullest.

Abena Johnson

Abena has been writing poetry and stories since she learned how to put a sentence together. Her passion was always with poetry. Her childhood has been rough and her way of expressing herself, like many artists and writers, was through her work.

Aaliyah J.

Aaliyah Jones is a 17-year-old high school senior from Houston, Texas. She enjoys writing as a form of self-expression and finds social issues to be the highlight of her pieces.

aisha khan

Aisha is a freshman in high school from Virginia. She is the daughter of a Pakistani immigrant and is developing an appreciation for heritage through literature. Aisha hopes to learn her way around the world through poetry.

Abigail Jade Koerner

Abigail Jade Koerner is the proud product of DC Public Schools. She began her education at Harvard University in the fall of 2017- studying Statistics, the Classics, and Mandarin Chinese. At Harvard, Abigail rows crew and volunteers with PBHA.

Janell Lee

Janell Lee is from Montclair, NJ, where she lives with her mom. She's a soon to be college student at Hofstra University, studying pre-vet science & art. In the future, Janell really wants to help out in any way she can, no matter how small.

Lillian G. Lewis

Born and raised in North Carolina, Lillian has always loved the arts. Outside of writing, her hobbies include singing and playing guitar. She's an upcoming sophomore at Athens Drive High School. This is her first published piece.

LSimoneM

LSimoneM is a native of Chicago pursuing her lifelong dream to become a writer. In 2016, she received a certificate in Grant Writing from DePaul University to begin her new life journey.

Shamiika Mitchell

Her journey in this life is to share and teach compassion, hope and love through written words that cannot be expressed orally. She is a 41-year-old, African American women, married, a mother of 7 children, and has 5 grandchildren.

Pauline Monter

Born in the Philippines and having immigrated at 7, Pauline fell in love with the impact of poetry, even though she once saw words as weakness. Now she hopes to share their beauty. She also spent about 40 minutes trying to figure out what to write for this bio.

Stella Mpisi

Stella Mpisi is a Congolese-born (Democratic Republic of Congo) South African writer and blogger. Her writing focuses on African socio-economic and cultural issues, colorism, and general struggles of growing up as an orphan.

Subbi Namakula

Subbi Namakula is an emerging poet; her work focuses on her language and country of Uganda. She is currently studying in the creative writing program at the University of Iowa.

Sabrina M. Pyun

Sabrina Pyun is currently a Writing Seminars student at Johns Hopkins University. She is a lover and writer of fiction and poetry and aspires to publish a book in the future! She shares her work and articles on her twitter @sabrinampyun.

Gladis Isabel Ricaurte

Gladis Isabel Ricaurte is a Colombian-born American author, who recently discovered poetry as a part of her writing profile. Her goal is to remind those who feel they are alone that they are not, and that writing is a medium of healing.

Krithika Shrinivas

Krithika Shrinivas is a high school student from New Jersey. She is an avid writer and uses poetry as a creative outlet. She has gained recognition for her writing, and loves to involve herself in literary pursuits.

Elizabeth Upshur

Elizabeth Upshur is an African American Southern poet, translator, and memoirist. Her poetry has been published in regional journals and is forthcoming in the anthology Africanization and Americanization. She has won several awards including the 2016 MLK, Jr., Essay Contest. She is a graduate student and freshman composition teacher at Western Kentucky University.

Tajinnea Wilson

Tajinnea, is a Creative Writing major at Susquehanna University. She's always had a passion for storytelling, but film is her true love. After graduation, she plans to pursue a career in the film industry as a screenwriter.

Edoka Writes

Edoka Writes is a published author, art curator, and cofounder of iN-DStudios—a creative hub for independent artists located in Atlanta. Edoka attended Kennesaw State University for creative writing and is currently studying script writing.

Reflection

Discussion Questions

After reading the book, readers and facilitators may use the following questions in multiple ways: group discussions, individual written responses, or personal reflection.

For the Collection

1. What were some of your favorite essays or poems in the anthology and why?

2. Which pieces, if any, seem out of place or inappropriate for the theme? Why do you think so?

3. Which selections remind you of your own experiences or observations of colorism? What did you think or feel while reading them?

4. Which selections express opinions, viewpoints, or experiences that are different from your own? What did you think or feel while reading them?

5. Do these pieces, individually or collectively, do a good job of addressing colorism? Why or why not?

6. Do any of the pieces seem to contradict each other? How so? What might such contradictions mean in defining, discussing, and addressing colorism?

7. What do you make of the fact that most of the selections in this anthology were written by girls or women? How might sex and gender matter when gathering or reading stories about colorism? How would this anthology be different if it included more male voices?

8. This volume includes writers of different races, ethnicities, and nationalities. What similarities or differences do you notice across different identities?

9. What other major themes appear in the book? How are those themes connected to the overarching theme of colorism?

10. Which of the essays or poems in this book give you the greatest sense of empowerment and hope for colorism healing, and why?

11. If you were to publish a book about colorism, what would it be like? How might it be similar to or different from *Colorism Essays and Poems*?

For Individual Pieces

1. What is the main idea of this essay/poem? How does the main idea relate to the issue of colorism?

2. Who or what is the speaker/narrator of this selection? What is the speaker's tone throughout the piece? Does the tone and mood of the piece seem effective in expressing the main idea? Why or why not?

3. What symbols or imagery seem important for developing the main idea, and why?

4. Do any significant shifts in character, tone, mood, or style occur in the piece? Why and how do these changes occur?

5. Which aspects of the essay or poem do you most identify with? Which parts do you least identify with or have questions about?

6. What other important themes besides colorism appear in this selection? How do all the themes connect or overlap?

Writing Prompts

The following prompts encourage deeper personal reflection on the issue of colorism, self-love, and the content of this anthology. You may choose to revise, edit, and polish your writing to submit as a school assignment, future contest entry, or publication online or in print. You might also prefer to simply keep them as personal journal entries.

Descriptive Writing

A. Look at yourself in a mirror or in a clear photograph. Do a free-write of what you see. Don't worry about spelling, grammar, punctuation, or structure as you free-write. When you think you've covered all the basics or reach a stopping point, begin again. Zoom in on the details. Use specific language. Use all five senses. Avoid generic terms like "light" or "dark."

B. Continue your description by going beyond the visual image of you. Describe the parts of you— your personality, character, thoughts, dreams, culture, identity, hobbies, unique quirks—that are deeper than your physical or external appearance.

Notice what emotions you feel during this process. Once you've exhausted the details, carefully read what you've written. Mark statements that stand out to you as positive and write or speak the statement: "I accept this as my truth." Then mark statements that feel negative, and write or speak the affirmation: "I forgive my negative perception, and I choose self-love instead."

Repeat this exercise as often as you like. Compare versions of your self-description. How does each new version compare or contrast with previous versions?

Narrative Writing

Reflect on a specific time when you experienced or witnessed colorism. Communicate this experience in narrative or story form. Think about the following as you write the first draft:

- Who are the primary people involved in this incident (characters)?
- What particular things do they say (dialogue)?
- Where and when does this event occur (setting)?
- What feelings, emotions, or attitudes do you observe in yourself or others involved (mood and tone)?
- What actions do people take (or that happen naturally) and in what order (plot sequence)?
- What was or is the main theme, takeaway, conclusion, or lesson in this story (there may be more than one)?

Repeat this exercise as often as necessary as more memories occur to you and as new experiences or observations of colorism happen. Compare and contrast the narratives you write. Are there common characters? Common phrases that people speak, common settings, or themes? Pay attention to any patterns that appear. This information might provide insight into your triggers or negative situations you might avoid or change as you work toward colorism healing for yourself, your family, and community.

Poetic Writing

Using inspiration from any of the poetry in this book, write your own poem about colorism. Experiment with figurative language, such as similes, metaphors, or personification. Explore various options for style and structure like rhythm, repetition, or alliteration. Pay close attention to tone and mood. Try out different forms like sonnets, odes, song lyrics, or elegies. Repeat this exercise as you feel compelled. Consider trying different approaches or techniques each time.

If you are unfamiliar with any of the above terms or want to take your exploration of poetry even further, the Poetry Foundation offers a good online resource for students, adults, and educators: https://www.poetryfoundation.org/learn.

Analytical Writing

Analytical writing explains a subject by examining its basic parts in relationship to the whole. Much like doctors examine patients, writers analyze a subject by looking closely at various details, often including outside research, to discover information that allows them to draw certain conclusions. Here are a few ways you could write an analysis on the subject of colorism.

1. **Problem - Cause - Solution.** Think about colorism as a problem you would like to solve. Explain what colorism is and why it is problematic. Identify specific causes of colorism, and explain possible solutions that directly address the specific causes you have identified. When explaining possible solutions, consider who is responsible for implementing them (individuals, families, community leaders, teachers, etc.).

2. **Compare and Contrast.** Choose two or three of the essays or poems in the book and write about how they are similar to or different from each other. You might begin by explaining more obvious similarities and differences then dig deeper to uncover those that are less obvious. Consider the content of the poem, the experiences described, imagery and descriptions, use of creative language like metaphors or similes, and sound or structure elements like rhyme, repetition, rhythm, stanza and line breaks, etc.

3. **Argument and Persuasion.** Analysis does not always require an explicit argument, but arguments

should always result from good analysis. For this argument, think of a relatively recent news story or pop culture event you think is relevant to colorism. Make an argument about what actions, if any, should be taken in response to this incident. Who should respond and how? Thoroughly explain the situation and why the actions you propose are the best response. Also consider alternative positions. What would you say to those who disagree with your position? Include appropriate research, historical and contemporary context, and other elements to strengthen your argument. Think about how you might appeal to the reader's intellect, morals, and emotions, as well as how you might establish your own credibility through your writing.

Made in United States
North Haven, CT
19 October 2022

25654185R00064